SCHOLASTIC READER

LEVEL 1

50-250 WORDS

ANIMAL FAMILIES

By Peter and Connie Roop

SCHOLASTIC INC.

We take pride in a new family: Jennifer, Andrew, and Madeline.

Cover: © meunierd/Shutterstock, © Olgysha/Shutterstock,
© ilker canikligil/Shutterstock, © Liliya Kulianionak/Shutterstock,
© Mogens Trolle/Shutterstock

Page 1 © Richard Burn/Shutterstock; Page 3 © iStockphoto;
Page 4 © Ewan Chesser/ Shutterstock; Page 6 © iStockphoto; Page 8 © iStockphoto;
Page 10 © iStockphoto; Page 12 © dcwcreations/Shutterstock;
Page 14 © vilainecrevette/Shutterstock; Page 16 © iStockphoto;
Page 18 © iStockphoto; Page 20 © Janelle Lugge/Shutterstock;
Page 22 © Mariusz S. Jurgielewicz/Shutterstock; Page 24 © lobster20/Shutterstock;
Page 26 © iStockphoto; Page 28 © Lenkadan/Shutterstock;
Page 30 © terekhov igor/Shutterstock; Page 31 © iStockphoto;
Page 32 © Utekhina Anna/Shutterstock.

ISBN 978-0-545-38556-5

10 9 8 7 6 5 4 3 2 1   12 13 14 15 16 17/0

Printed in the U.S.A.   40
First printing, September 2012

Many
ANIMALS
live in groups.

LIONS

sleep in prides.

WOLVES

hunt in packs.

GEESE fly in flocks.

ELEPHANTS

graze in herds.

BEES

buzz in swarms.

FISH
swim in schools.

TOADS
hop in knots.

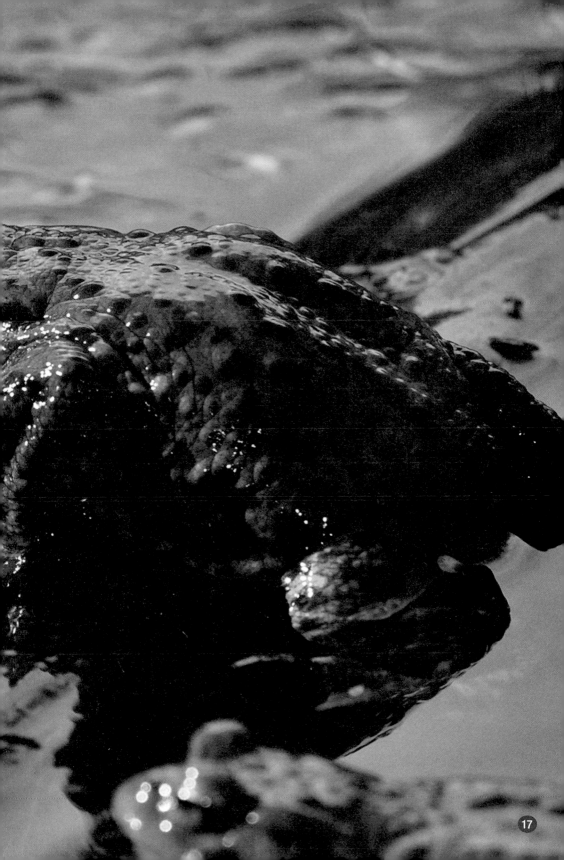

KANGAROOS
jump in mobs.

CATERPILLARS

eat in armies.

JELLYFISH

drift in smacks.

DUCKS
paddle in rafts.

ANTS
work in colonies.

PUPPIES
play in litters.

CHICKS

peck in peeps.

You eat, sleep, play, work, and live in a **FAMILY**.

GLOSSARY

Drift: to float slowly in water

Graze: to eat grass while moving

Hunt: to search for food

Paddle: to move through the water by moving one's feet

Peck: to pick up food with a beak